My Weight Of Being

Thoughts between the said and unsaid

Tripura Ranade Arora

Made with ❤ on the BookLeaf Publishing Platform
www.bookleafpub.in
www.bookleafpub.com

Dedication

To my son Kaavya,

You are my poetry in motion,
the animation of my every feeling....
The best rhyme that life has offered,
in carrying the weight of my being.....

Preface

My Weight of Being is an exploration of everything we bear to endure the journey of life. While we learn to toughen up, we often forget the beauty in being softer. We continue to carry weights, sometimes even when they're no longer needed. Finally, I realised, the beauty of letting go never makes us weaker; it makes us stronger. And here I am sharing my journey!

This collection of thoughts is an invitation into the most intimate corners of my soul, where grief, hope, love, pity, and doubts reside—our constant companions on the road to self-discovery.

As you flip these pages, I hope you find yourself not only in the words but in the spaces between them: the things we know but never say, and the things we don't know, which still manage to find their way into expression.

May you come to recognize the weight of your own being, the unseen burdens you carry. To find the moments when, like me, you are ready, simply let go. In each poem, I offer my two cents of understanding, about life as I know it!

This is my journey. These are my weights. I invite you to share them, to carry them with me, if only for a moment—before we find the strength to release them together.

Acknowledgements

This book reflects my life journey, without which it would have been a stack of empty pages. So, thanks to life for enriching me with experiences.

Thanking my family will never feel enough! They have been patient with me, offering unwavering support. We all pushed our limits to carry "my weight of being." They heard the drafts, redrafts, and encouraged me to keep going, believing in me every step of the way.

To my friends, who have inspired me and pulled me through this new endeavor. Special thanks to Prithvi, for the timely checks and for reminding me that I am going to make it!

Lastly, to my readers—thank you for allowing me to share my story. May these poems offer you a moment of reflection and perhaps solace.

This book wouldn't have come to life without the support of those who believed in me, both in silence and in action.

1. Unburdened

We all carry things no one can see. Some stay longer than they should. But the heaviest weight is often deciding when to put them down—isn't it?

I have carried the weight of yesterday,
My pockets full of stones—too heavy to throw.
Clinging to each wrong turn as a marker,
Making the path ahead painfully slow.

I have counted my faults like endless stars,
Too many, too bright, too distant to erase.
Wandered through galaxies of self-blame,
Craving the warmth of a tender embrace.

I stand today, a reshaped soul,
Ghosted my past I no longer own.
The journey spiralled like a rabbit hole,
Never swift, but still, I have flown.

I have learned to seek peaceful, quiet spaces;

To breathe, to sit, to let go, and release.
Pain lingers; doesn't vanish with a blink,
Yet in the calm, my soul settles in ease.

Today, I whisper to my heart: "It's time to let go."
Just live, like you were always meant to heal....
Enough of picking battles with yourself;
Trust me, it was never that big of a deal......

2. Illusion of "Me"

We try to shape life with our hopes. But when hopes shift, life reshapes. I wonder—are we truly designing, or simply playing our part in the cosmic play?

I always imagined a life in my mind,
But serenity slipped past—silent, unkind.

Love found me, not sure how or why,
Then vanished one morning, without a goodbye.

A lone wolf I turned, howling at the moon,
Dancing to a tune that ended too soon.

Joy hid away while sorrow took its toll,
Tears watched life gnaw pieces from my soul.

Yet in the dark, hope sparked its light,
Clinging to faith with all its might.

I can't deny, some prayers found their way,

But most were abandoned, to wander astray.

Life weaved complexity, part cruel, part kind,
Far from the one I envisioned in mind.

Now I let go of versions, once deemed mine,
Patiently wait, and let time redesign.

3. Excess Baggage

If our brain decides to go on a vacation, what do you think it will pack? Will it travel light or just pay for excess baggage?

I planned a holiday for my brain,
A forced gift, with much to explain.

It was overdue, let's admit and say—
A mental vacay always pushed away.

Half-heartedly, my brain got ready,
Packed a bag, unexpectedly heavy.

I saw it exceed the weight limit—
In that tiny space, what all was fit?

I opened the suitcase, with great dismay,
Stunned by the view, with nothing to say.

Anxiety subtly wanted to carry all chaos,

It settled on top, controlling every toss.

Stress was crammed in, along with worry,
Overthinking sprawled, without a hurry.

Ifs and buts stuffed on the side,
Should-haves happily joined the ride.

Regret nearly filled every crack,
Stills and yets made their own stack.

So much was packed, yet more remained,
Old thoughts, half-healed, still unexplained.

With one deep breath, I zipped the suitcase,
This baggage seems... a bottomless mess.

So I postponed the vacay, to "Some" day,
Realizing I'm the one not ready for the getaway.

My brain just winked, "Well, now you see—
You can't escape what you've packed within me."

4. The Remainder

*They often say what remains is greater than what is lost.
But in your persistent absence, can that ever truly be
true?*

One day you were gone,
vanished in thin air,
Like a step was missed
from my routine stair.

No warning, no hint
you're nowhere to be found,
Yet I search endlessly
for your touch, your sound.

I move on to each day
with your memory as my guide,
Yet I walk hollow,
filled with eternal void inside.

Eventually, I return to joy,

celebrations to claim,
But your empty seat reminds me
it's never the same.

The years pass by,
and I learn to wear a smile,
But your absence lingers
with me all this while.

You closed your ledger,
pure and defined,
Which knots to untie,
I'm still trying to find.

Through unending trials,
I look for my contribution:
A remainder in your equation,
just waiting, for a solution...

5. When Silence Talks....

In a world crowded with gestures, souls often lose their way, measuring love through gestures alone. But does a soulmate really need proof?

We talk, we share, we intertwine,
We're older together, like vintage wine

Yet what I cherish most is this—
Locking eyes, sending touchless kiss.

A bond so deep, beyond all frames,
Dissolving selves, yet mingling names.

The way your breath aligns with mine,
Sends my pulse dancing up the spine.

The way you light up when I'm near,
Outshines pretentious flowers we revere.

While others waltz through chatty sound,

Our quiet talks stay deep, not bound.

In this golden silence, we flirt and tease,
No restless urge to try or please.

This silence isn't a void or lack,
Where hearts undress and feelings unpack.

Our story is now beyond words,
Loving our path, unlike the herds.

So talk we may, and talk we must,
Comfortably, in silence lives our trust.

We dream and share vision beyond sight,
Drenched in quiet love, from dusk to twilight.

6. Alibis for Life

He believed in me before I did and I've been catching up
ever since.
How does someone so little become such a big part of
our life?

He looks up slow, "You trust me, right?"
With chocolate smudged across his cheek.
Resolved the ice-cream emergency with swords,
Like every midnight mission, bold, not meek.

I placed the last pillow, the fort stood tall,
And gave war cries, with snacks in hand.
The couch became his royal hall,
As plastic knights marched to Alexa's band.

We strategize to save his favorite dinos,
From a world so loud, so harsh, so cruel.
We spend our hours in wits and puns,
Each comeback scored like it's a duel.

He says, "I didn't do it," with teary eyes,
And his cheeks turned a bashful pink.
I shrug a shoulder, slow and sly,
Then hide the torn diary with subtle wink.

We talk, we listen, we fight, we cry,
Then cuddle close for end-of-day check-ins.
We giggle, we sob, sulk till teardrops dry,
Grunt through pillow fights, sorting losses and wins.

Someday he'll give up swords and capes,
Trade dino-saving for real-life stress.
But I'll be guarding his fort with ice cream,
As home is a feeling, and I'll be his address.

7. An Idea of You

In the quest for ideal love, we let the mind sculpt one for
us.
Maybe it isn't what we need — maybe it's only what we
think we do.
Who can ever know?

I wasn't there when your tale began,
Yet I ink your ending, as only I can.

With borrowed truths and stitched-up ends,
I chase an idea my mind defends.

I'm aware you're a feeling, not a fact,
Yet my heart still rushes to react.

In your silence, I search for hints,
Read every pause, tracing your prints.

Wrapped in the silhouette of maybe,
I fall for a man crafted by me.

I celebrate your mum as proficiency,
Ignore the cracks in your consistency.

I try to blame fate, perhaps poor timing,
Still wait for a perfect celestial chiming.

I hold your hand in thoughts that stay,
And wish you'd pull, not drift away.

Not just in dreams, but I hope you'll be
The kind who stays — who chooses me.

I exhale "someday" and continue to pray
Knowing this love won't see the light of day.

I know my delusions. I know what's true.
Still, I stay in love with the idea of you.

8. Duel to Dual

*We try to paint the world in black and white. But often,
the mind just speaks what the heart already knows.
Then, are they truly different, or just two tones uttering
the same words?*

Logic showed up, sharp and neat,
With slides, pointers, and a data sheet.

Intuition slipped in, confident but wild,
No script, no plan, just the inner child.

Logic drew lines. Intuition swayed.
One built the plan. The other disobeyed.

Intuition ran barefoot on grass,
Logic rolled eyes, refused to let it pass.

Intuition holds *why*, Logic clings to *how*,
I'm torn: if to dream, or live in *now*.

Logic tap-danced to beats of precision,
Intuition performed with chaotic vision.

They circle me like rivals for life,
A tug-of-war on the edge of a knife.

I'm stuck between their light and fire,
Holding both my doubt and desire.

Amid the fight, I call for a truce.
I stand firm, won't choose or lose.

I'll honor the reason and the rhyme,
Happily break rules—but check the time.

I borrow sense, I borrow spark,
I pave my way through light and dark.

Some days I walk a measured line,
And some days I leap and claim it mine.

"To be" is not to split the thread!
But braid the heart and mind instead.

I give up sides, just to bear the strain,
Embrace the duel—and together, remain.

9. Hello, Goodbye and Nothing!

*When the ache between the said and unheard begins to
echo, we realize loneliness isn't the absence of people,
but presence unmet.
And I wonder, could solitude be the best company after
all?*

I am knitting words from lessons I've learned,
Still tasting the ash of bridges that burned.

A chipped cup holds me with quiet and tea,
While feelings stir, desperate to flee.

The clock ticks sharp on the gloomy wall,
I turn away, hoping daylight will stall.

My pen marks down every quiet defeat,
Tiptoeing through sorrow with cautious feet.

I crave a space where the soul drops fear,

Each pause a plea, each tremble a tear.

I needed no cure, no advice to smolder—
Room in your head and a wrap on my shoulder.

We sit closer, with your long-lost eyes,
You listen to me with meaningless sighs.

You sip your drink with eyes on the screen,
Your "Tell me more" feels cold and routine.

I realize this talk holds no connection,
Hollow action, without intention.

Still I nod, I smile, I play along—
Chatter swells, but silence grows strong.

You leave with a kiss, light as air,
And take nothing from the weight I bare.

When your footsteps quickly vanish,
I hold myself, too bruised to banish.

I go numb, let the chaos blur,
And return to my solitude—even emptier.

10. No Room to Rent

Most of us are more agile than we think. We find
comfort even in discomfort when it's familiar.
We name it life. Because why not?

Grief moved in one day, totally uncalled,
Carrying bags full of tears and sighs.
She calimed to be easy, low maintenance,
With an opaque face and empty eyes.

She settles in, claims the master bed,
Uses my things without hesitation.
Critiques each corner, every spread,
Muttering, "I had no expectation."

Eats my food straight from the fridge,
She asks, "Don't you have a job?"
Glances at tissues strewn near the bed,
And rolls her eyes at each frail sob.

She never bothers to help with chores,

Secretly wishing for messier mess.
She deals a hand of mind games, though,
Leaving me lost, purely just to guess.

She frames my regrets across the wall,
Binge-watches my breakdowns like a show.
I try to console myself into peace,
Leaves sarcastic reviews: "Too fast—go slow."

Without much choice, I let her stay,
We just cohabit, awkward yet tight.
I ignore her most irritating tricks,
As she hummed lullabies on sleepless night.

I softly requested her to leave,
Then tried yoga, pills, prayer, and walks.
She just kept coming back magically,
Even after changing every single lock.

I plan to co-sign a lease with her,
She was never a guest but a part of me.
I realise the locks never really mattered,
As I had handed her the only key.

11. Futile Knock

When people matter, we hold on—often without an answer. It takes strength to stay, but even more to let go. The real trick, knowing when and how. Isn't it?

I knocked with hope, not fear or pride,
With a faint faith to be loved inside.

With each knock, my truth unwound,
Hoping for an eager mirrored sound.

I wasn't bothered by shape or frame,
A quench to connect made all surfaces same.

I dropped my mask, guards, no disguise,
Believing others would be ready likewise.

I was dressed in "me", my best costume,
And watched dead soil, waited for bloom.

I looked harder for a knob or a hinge,

Found a stony wall that refused to singe.

I knocked because I dared to care—
But not all souls can meet you there.

So I walked away—not torn, not hurt,
Just clear on what is truly worth the effort.

And next time, when I'm bound to call,
I'll knock with care—on doors, not wall.

12. About Time

Nature abhors a vacuum. So naturally, we fill our minds
—thoughts, memories, noise.
But is it worth what it costs us to hoard?

I opened the cupboard tucked in my head—
Stuffed with the silence of words once left unsaid.

The drawer below held feelings once stashed,
Still seeking validation, eager to be rehashed.

It's spilling wide with old pains and regrets,
Uncomfortable adjustments hang from half-shut chests.

An unused smile folded, packed away neat,
A clear "no" choked, struggling to beat.

Letters well-written, unaddressed in a tray,
Afraid they'd go naked if sent on their way.

Discarded dreams, now biting the dust,

Too fragile to open, corroded by rust.

Overwhelmed by the mess I uncover,
Why I kept it at all—I start to wonder.

I'll gift this mess a beautiful wake,
And give up my hoarding—for my own sake.

It hurts to let go, but it hurts more to keep,
What ruins my mornings and poisons my sleep.

It's time to let life take its rightful turn,
Declutter my mind, let it simply unlearn.

13. Almost

I'm shaped by bittersweet endings and the tang of
unfinished business. Achievements are fine, but it's the
incompletions that have taught me most.
Ever wondered... if fate procrastinates too?

I reached for flame, it knew my name,
Then served me up a cold roast.
The warmth was real, my skin confessed
Did I get burned? ... almost.

I poured my heart into the pages,
Wallowed in pride, not meant to post.
The ink ran drier than my tears
Did someone read? ... almost.

I rowed a canoe through meaning's sea,
Even with a map, I missed the coast.
I tried to dodge an unseen iceberg
Did I reach the shore? ... almost.

I had a fairytale blooming bright,
A charming prince, my perfect host.
But fate recast me as the vamp
Did my ending change? ... almost.

I built a ladder to my oblivion,
My past returned, a haunting ghost.
I crumbled there with frightened eyes
Did I rise again? ... almost.

I now have a quilt stitched with "almosts",
It keeps me warm, and humbles boast.
It taught me to love both beauty and scars
Did I survive life? ... almost.

14. Solo Trip

The journey inward is as thrilling as the outward one—
only, no two itineraries look alike. And when you return,
you bring back more than souvenirs. So, get set, go?

A golden hush begins to drip,
Beyond the blur of thought and sleep.
Carefree winds send silent invites,
On fog-wrapped roads, charms to keep.

The trees dress in rustles and gushes,
Leaves bathe in fragrant light.
Bright hilltops allure from far away,
A strange but welcoming sight.

The soothing breeze makes it cozy,
The sun turns soft behind a cloud.
It flirts with me and offers chance,
Draping the path like surreal shroud.

I need no bag, no route to follow,

No plan to bind my mind.
Yet I pause, doing aftermath,
Afraid of what I'll find.

I sought for signs from far above,
Then look at the home I own.
One foot in and one foot out!
Thrilled yet worried, on cusp of unknown.

Will walking on make me a runaway,
Fleeing from my chosen role?
Is that just escape dressed as need,
Or reclaiming my lost soul?

While reaching out for hands to hold,
I bargain a counter plea—
Why long for steps that walk beside,
When this was not meant to be?

I gently wave back, I pack myself,
Stop asking for signs or guarantee.
I embrace my first step outside,
On the path to reach, destination me

15. Butterfly Effect

*They say one small flutter can start a storm.I say it
already did, in my mind, because it notices!
My fellow overthinkers, do we agree?*

I notice every minor spark,
I hear each hum before it's dark.

My heartbeat stumbles, quick and dumb!
At things the others choose to go numb.

An expression, a pause, a breath held tight,
Can turn the calmest day to chaotic night.

I revisit all my jokes, assess and scale,
Maybe it landed, but was my delivery stale?

Turning in my bed, I replay each conversation,
Was I too harsh? Did I skip some explanation?

I replace answers with more question marks!

Thoughts chew their tail, with restless barks.

I end up giving more , I overshare, I overcare,
Till I run empty, compelled only to self-repair.

I function, I turn on the outer calm mode,
While thoughts fire shots, always set to reload.

Then a misfit reply beeps, off what I feel vital,
And my rebel thoughts begin to spiral...

One butterfly flaps wings beneath my skin,
Unleashing a thought-tsunami stirring within.

It left my palms, without trace of colors,
I longed, but was only meant for others.

It came, then vanished—ignored my request,
Gifted me endless flutter, shaking my unrest.

16. Goal Post

I like rules. They aren't fun, but they are a must. Trust
me, they were never meant to be broken... by me.
But what if life changes them anyway?

I am told to do what is right, always,
Color between the lines only, for praise.

If I outgrew the box, I might get thrown,
So I live by meek rules I never could own.

I by heart the books till their pages wear thin,
Each page a command I am told to seed in.

No stumbles, no falls, hurdles are for embrace,
Calculated swift steps, just to stay in the race.

Stitching my breaths to their measured schemes,
Learning to envision just regular dreams.

Just when I crown myself, to have it all,

Time stands still, and begins to stall.

I search for the wins I thought were in store,
But life has moved past keeping that score.

I played by the book, yet it was in vain,
As life moved the goalpost once again.

Why let some yardstick crawl over my skin,
When it's never the game I meant to begin....

17. Redrawn Island

A line drawn is not always a wall. Sometimes, it's where
we truly belong.
How for must we go to return to ourselves?

Once there was a singing shore,
Loved by sails and kissed by sand;
Laughter and hope crowned every crest,
Offering fruit to every hand.

It harboured both the wild and wind,
And blessed each passing waft;
Welcoming ships with open arms,
A home for anchor and for raft.

Rains created some havoc,
Stripped the hope from every strand;
Hollowed the shore, like it belonged,
Leaving behind a lonely land.

Then walls rose from salted stones,

Marking where trust had bled;
The tides rushed in, then faded out,
As the heart learned how to tread.

Now the shore is an island,
Afar, aloof, and perfectly broken;
Awaits the right one to ride the storms,
Finding its truth, not merely open.

So now tides may come and go,
Defined horizon guards its land;
The island enjoys its own being,
Even at the cost of being unmanned.

18. Happily Ever After

No one is promised a perfect ending. We chase it anyway
— hearts bruised, dreams bent, but ready to re-do.
Isn't that its own kind of faith?

We all chase pretty but fragile bubbles,
Reach for safe paths, away from known troubles.

A life where wishes rise without inner churn,
Where sorrow is dodged with a swift U-turn.

A road that's smooth, with signs well-lit,
No sudden falls, no walls to hit.

Where every "maybe" becomes surreal,
And frail softer dreams begin to congeal.

Can we really draft a flawless script,
Where no detail fades, no meanings drift?

The perfect end to a perfect tale might be ajar,

A mirage we chase, from star to star.

The price of wisdom is heavy and steep,
Trading moments for experience to keep.

It was the "chase," the art all along,
Enriching me, gifting a sense to belong.

Rebellious hope, fuels to turn a new chapter,
Igniting the quest for a happily ever after.

19. In the Name of Love

In the quest of being loved, we simply mend our ways.
Love is not blind, but it is blinding, for sure.
But is that blindness eternal?

I replaced my every opinion
with a pick-me silence,
Wondered if my being around
held silky, subtle balance.
I avoided the rise, savoured the fall,
Call it love? Or nothing at all.

I practiced patience with care,
Lent warmth, mastering that art.
Left spaces between my fingers wide,
Offering comfort to heal a heart.
Wanted to shatter, yet stood tall,
Call it love? Or nothing at all.

Each "no" returned with a raised brow,

A sigh, hinting me to adjust.
I bowed down unknowingly,
To escape the ache of eerie disgust.
Kept tuning, absorbing my inner brawl,
Call it love? Or nothing at all.

Drowning in conflicting thoughts,
I kept hoping for something more.
A murmur gently leaned in:
How far I've drifted from my core.
To walk away or to stall?
Call it love? Or nothing at all.

Torn and aware, I stand on the edge,
Realizing, "I am enough."
I choose to live within my skin,
No longer bound by being tough.
Saying it out loud won't make me small,
It will be called "Love" after all!

20. The Cruel One

We provide the raw material, and nostalgia constructs a
world. A silent co-passenger on our journey.
But what if, one day, it becomes the driver?

Nostalgia is cruel, wrapped in velvet disguise,
Slowly opening the memory jar, freeing fireflies.

It stirs the air, sprays perfume from the past,
You're drawn to the scent, but it doesn't last.

You gulp the laugh, then choke on a tear,
Tap on the dance steps you once held dear.

Some memories bloom, while others decay,
With your exhale, the present is stolen away.

You can't resist, indulging in a peek,
Exposing your soul, heart broken and weak.

Each lane that you walk, is built on lies,

A maze of shattered dreams and mute goodbyes.

The maze is endless, feeding on your pain,
The exit is a myth, just toying with your brain.

You beg to get out, but exit is sealed,
Peeling skin from the wound still not healed.

Nostalgia snaps fingers, and the show goes on,
Running through memory lane, just like a pawn.

He can lock you up in the world he bestows,
Winning every time, with all that he knows!

21. Potion of Immortality

We wish to get out of circle of life, but we end up
seeking immortality in legacy, memory, or the very
essence of time. We create more open ends, in trying to
close a few.
Isn't the loop just infinite?

I don't dream of living long,
Not on tombstone or in a song.

Not as ash, residing in an urn,
Not as a legend for children to learn.

But still, I long for a subtle trace,
A carving, "I was here," claiming my place.

Occasionally, my name softly spoken,
A heart that holds a memory, as a token.

In thirst to not be fully gone,
I brew a potion, to forever linger on.

What if wisdom's not to stay forever?
Exit per plan, even if the play isn't over.

No legacy, no shrine, no hall of fame,
Uniting with infinity, that's the end game.

Do I want to vanish or stay behind?
I'm tangled, yet I'm ready to unwind.

I too leave back, unanswered 'to be or not to be?'
I sip or don't, the potion still gives me, my eternity.